SEAWEED

Nature's FRIENDS

by Joyce Markovics

NORWOOD HOUSE PRESS

NORWOOD HOUSE 🏠 PRESS

For more information about Norwood House Press, please visit our website at: www.norwoodhousepress.com or call 866-565-2900.

Book Designer: Ed Morgan
Editorial and Production: Bowerbird Books

Photo Credits: Wikimedia Commons, cover; freepik.com, title page; © iStock.com/fdastudillo, 4; Wikimedia Commons, 5; Wikimedia Commons, 6; © iStock.com/Michael Zeigler, 7; LJ/Unsplash.com, 8; Wikimedia Commons, 9; © iStock.com/inusuke, 10–11; © iStock.com/Natalie Ruffing, 12; © iStock.com/Velvetfish, 13 left; © iStock.com/VargaJones, 13 right; © iStock.com/spiderment, 14; © iStock.com/Michael Zeigler, 16; © iStock.com/juanmoro, 15; © iStock.com/Michael Zeigler, 16; © iStock.com/JJ van Ginkel, 17; freepik.com, 18; freepik.com, 19; © iStock.com/Alexisaj, 20; © iStock.com/kerriekerr, 21; freepik.com, 22; freepik.com, 23; © iStock.com/spiderment, 24; © iStock.com/MattStansfield, 27; © iStock.com/Michael Zeigler, 29.

Hardcover ISBN: 978-1-68450-764-1
Paperback ISBN: 978-1-68404-779-6

Library of Congress Cataloging-in-Publication Data
Names: Markovics, Joyce L., author.
Title: Seaweed / by Joyce Markovics.
Description: Chicago : Norwood House Press, [2023] | Series: Nature's friends | Includes bibliographical references and index. | Audience: Grades 2-3
Identifiers: LCCN 2022000257 (print) | LCCN 2022000258 (ebook) | ISBN 9781684507641 (hardcover) | ISBN 9781684047796 (paperback) | ISBN 9781684047857 (ebook)
Subjects: LCSH: Marine algae--Juvenile literature. | Marine algae--Climatic factors--Juvenile literature. | Marine algae as food--Juvenile literature.
Classification: LCC QK570.2 .M39 2023 (print) | LCC QK570.2 (ebook) | DDC 579.8/177--dc23/eng/20220111
LC record available at https://lccn.loc.gov/2022000257
LC ebook record available at https://lccn.loc.gov/2022000258

353N—082022

Manufactured in the United States of America in North Mankato, Minnesota.

CONTENTS

UNDERWATER FOREST

Beneath the Pacific Ocean is a forest unlike any other. It's made up of kelp, a type of seaweed! Kelp can be as tall as some trees—up to 115 feet (35 m). It can also grow up to a foot in one day. Kelp has thick, yellow-green leaflike parts called blades. As the ocean water moves, the blades sway like giant ribbons.

Sea otters swim above a kelp forest.

Lots of creatures find food and protection in kelp forests. Countless animals—from snails to sea otters—live there. For example, sea otters feed and raise their young in the swaying seaweed. However, Pacific kelp forests are under attack. Their enemies are spiky, purple, and very hungry.

This kelp forest is off the coast of California. However, kelp forests grow around the world.

When they sleep, sea otters wrap their bodies in kelp. It keeps them from drifting out to sea.

The kelp attackers are purple sea urchins. In 2013, huge numbers of sunflower sea stars died. These giant starfishes are as big as car tires. One of their favorite foods is purple sea urchins. Then, in 2014, unusually warm water called "the Blob" swept into the kelp forests. As a result, the water temperature rose above normal. This stressed the animals living there.

A sunflower sea star

Purple sea urchins have round shells covered with spines. They often live on the ocean floor.

The urchin **population** exploded. Soon, they covered the seafloor like a pointy purple carpet. They feasted on the kelp. "Sometimes we see dozens of them crawling up the stem of the kelp and taking it down from there," said one scientist. The urchins turned the forest into a wasteland.

Experts aren't sure what caused "the Blob." Ocean warming due to climate change could be to blame.

SEAWEED FACTS

Despite their appearance, kelp and other seaweeds are not plants. Rather, they're types of algae. Algae are living things that grow in fresh and salt water. Seaweeds are also not weeds as their name suggests. Most grow along seashores in dense patches. That's why people often see clumps of seaweed washed up on a beach.

Seaweed called green sea fingers on a beach

A kelp's holdfast torn from the seafloor after a storm

Seaweeds don't have roots. Some attach themselves to the seafloor or rocks using holdfasts. Holdfasts look like tangles of spaghetti. Much like their name, they "hold" seaweed "fast" in place. Other seaweeds float on the surface of the sea. They look like big rafts bobbing in the ocean.

Seaweeds have one major thing in common with plants. They use the Sun's energy to make their own food. This process is called photosynthesis (foh-tuh-SIN-thuh-siss). Seaweeds **harness** sunlight to take in **carbon dioxide**. Then they turn it into food. As they do, they release **oxygen**. In fact, seaweeds produce twenty percent of the oxygen in Earth's **atmosphere**!

Seaweeds make a portion of the oxygen that people breathe.

Seaweeds grow close to the surface to reach the Sun's light.

As a result of people burning fuel, there's much more carbon dioxide in the atmosphere and ocean. Seaweeds capture millions of tons of carbon dioxide. This equals as much carbon as New York State makes in one year! Also, when seaweeds die, they lock away carbon in their **tissues**. Experts are looking into how to sink some types of kelp to the ocean floor. When stored deep underwater, the carbon can't harm the planet. In these ways, seaweeds are fighting climate change.

MANY KINDS

There are three main types of seaweeds: brown, red, and green. Kelp is one of 1,500 kinds of brown seaweeds. Brown seaweeds are common in cold water. What sets them apart from other seaweeds are their pneumatocysts (noo-MAT-uh-sists). These are round pods filled with air. They act like tiny balloons. They allow the leaflike blades of kelp, for example, to float upright in the water. As a result, the seaweed can access more sunlight. This helps with photosynthesis.

Kelp pneumatocysts

Sargassum is another type of brown seaweed. It has berry-like pneumatocysts. It floats in huge patches on the ocean's surface. Patches of sargassum can stretch for miles. They provide food, homes, and places for creatures to raise young. These include birds, fish, turtles, and shrimp. Some, like the sargassum fish, spend their whole lives in the floating seaweed.

Sargassum fish blend into their seaweed home.

Sargassum seaweed floating in the ocean

Stringy acid kelp, a type of brown seaweed, has a chemical weapon. When fish try to eat it, it releases acid!

Red seaweeds far outnumber brown. Many of the 4,100 kinds grow on other living things, such as plants and corals. Coralline algae are a kind of seaweed that help build coral reefs. Small sea animals called polyps (POL-ips) ooze minerals that form coral reefs. However, coralline algae grow as a crust over the coral. In this way, the algae "glue" the reefs together.

Coralline algae

Green seaweed is the smallest group. Most green seaweeds grow in fresh water. Green fleece and hollow green are two types. Green fleece grows as bushy branches. Some people think it looks like a cluster of green worms. Sea lettuces are another group of green algae. This bright green seaweed looks like lettuce in a salad!

Freshwater green seaweed

SEAWEED EATERS

Every type of seaweed is food for **marine** animals. Seaweed is an important part of the **food web**. For example, **invertebrates** graze on kelp blades. These creatures include snails, crabs, abalone, and sea urchins. Other animals, such as seals, sea otters, and gray whales, feed on the invertebrates. Each animal depends on the next to survive.

Seals in a kelp forest

Fish also take shelter in kelp forests and other seaweeds. They often raise their babies there. Seagulls, terns, and egrets catch fish living in seaweeds. Small birds feed off of seaweeds as well. They skim the water for flies, shrimp, and other small animals.

A seagull catches a crab.

Pieces of rotting kelp sink to the ocean depths. There, it provides food for deep-sea animals, such as worms and fish.

Seaweed salad

People also eat seaweed. About 145 kinds are used as food. Seaweed is full of vitamins and minerals. It's also tasty. In Asia, seaweed is an important part of a person's daily diet. Japanese people have been eating it for 1,500 years! They roll dried seaweed called nori around raw fish and rice. The result is sushi. Japanese people make a soup called dashi with seaweed, too.

Sushi rolls

In Iceland, people put seaweed in salads and bread. Irish people snack on seaweed as well. One variety known as carrageenan turns into jelly when boiled. It's used to thicken pudding and other foods. In fact, algae are added to more than seventy percent of all food items! These include ice cream, canned foods, and cookies.

Crackers made from seaweed

ALGAE ASSETS

In addition, people feed seaweed to farm animals. These animals include sheep, cows, and pigs. Some in coastal areas eat seaweed that washes up onshore. For other farm animals, farmers mix seaweed into their feed. Seaweed is very **nutritious**. It's also plentiful, grows fast, and is cheaper than many other livestock feeds.

A sheep eating seaweed

A seaweed farm

To keep up with demand, farmers grow seaweed all over the world. The largest seaweed farm in North America is off the coast of Alaska. There, farmers grow kelp on long lines in the ocean. When the blades reach 10 feet (3 m), they are gathered. As they grow, seaweeds keep ocean water clean and healthy. They can soak up **pollutants**. Seaweeds also absorb nutrients to stop deadly **algal blooms**.

Cows that eat seaweed burp and fart less methane! Methane is a gas that contributes to climate change.

Beyond food, seaweed is used in other items. There are small amounts of red seaweed in toothpaste and shampoo, for example. Brown seaweed is used in heartburn relief and other medicines. Seaweeds are also ingredients in makeup and paint.

Many varieties of toothpaste contain seaweed.

Seaweed is valuable to humans in yet another way. It can be made into fuel! Burning gas creates a lot of pollution. It also produces carbon dioxide that worsens climate change. However, seaweed absorbs carbon dioxide. Because it's grown in the ocean, it doesn't use up land, fresh water, or other **resources**. In the future, seaweed fuel could be a great source of clean energy.

Scientists test seaweed in a lab.

KELP UNDER THREAT

Some seaweeds are under serious threat. People create pollution that can kill seaweeds and slow their growth. Seaweeds are also impacted by climate change. Climate change warms the air and ocean. This makes it harder for certain animals to survive and easier for others that harm seaweeds.

Kelp that has been destroyed by urchins or other predators

In California's kelp forests, warmer waters led to a boom of purple sea urchins. Hungry urchins **devour** kelp. "They're kind of like zombies," says one scientist. Since 2014, ninety-five percent of kelp forests in northern California have disappeared. Scientists, including Michael Graham, are taking action. He's looking into farming and replanting the kelp. Divers are also collecting the urchins. Then the urchins are sold as food for people. Fewer urchins could help the forests regrow. Since 2014, the forests are showing signs of recovery.

As a result of climate change, there are many more strong storms. Storms can rip kelp from the seafloor and tear up kelp blades.

A WORLD WITHOUT SEAWEED

What if there were no seaweeds? All the creatures that depend on seaweeds could die. Humans would lose an important food source. There would also be much more carbon dioxide on Earth. The planet could heat up even more and, over time, be unsuitable for people.

So what can you do to help seaweeds? Every person can do something to slow climate change. For instance, use less energy by walking or riding a bike. Cut back on plastics and other waste that might end up in the ocean. Also, share what you learned in this book with others. Seaweeds are survivors. Given the right conditions, they can regrow before our eyes!

A diver swims through seaweed.

HELP KELP!

Kelp forests are in serious trouble. However, there are ways that you can help kelp. Look below to learn about how you can make a difference. Then choose one option—and do it!

- Create a poster that shows a healthy kelp forest versus one that is barren and only has purple sea urchins in it.
- Write a short speech telling your family and friends about kelp forests, what lives in them, and what would happen if we lost them forever.
- Do something to help reduce climate change. Make less waste at home or cut down on your energy use. For example, ask an adult to walk or bike with you instead of driving somewhere.

TAKE ACTION NOW.
KELP NEEDS YOUR HELP!

GLOSSARY

algae (AL-jee): plantlike living things, including seaweed, that grow in water.

algal blooms (AL-guhl BLOOMS): rapid growths of algae.

atmosphere (AT-muhss-fihr): the mixture of gases that surround Earth.

carbon dioxide (KAR-buhn dye-AHK-side): a colorless and odorless gas given off when things decay or are burned.

chemical (KEM-uh-kuhl): a natural or human-made substance.

climate change (KLYE-mit CHAYNJ): the warming of Earth's air and oceans due to environmental changes, such as a buildup of greenhouse gases that trap the sun's heat in Earth's atmosphere.

corals (KOR-uhlz): groups of rocklike structures formed from the skeletons of sea animals called polyps.

devour (di-VOUR): to eat hungrily and quickly.

food web (FOOD WEB): a system of interdependent plants and animals that rely on one another for food.

harness (HAR-niss): to capture.

invertebrates (in-VUR-tuh-brits): animals that don't have backbones.

marine (muh-REEN): having to do with the sea.

nutritious (noo-TRISH-uhs): healthful and nourishing.

oxygen (AHK-suh-juhn): an invisible gas found in water or air, which people and animals breathe.

pollutants (pu-LOO-tuhnts): substances that contaminate a place.

population (pop-yuh-LAY-shuhn): the number of people or animals living in a place.

resources (REE-sorss-iz): materials found in nature or made by humans.

tissues (TISH-ooz): groups of connected cells of the same type inside a living thing.

FOR MORE INFORMATION

Books

Blanchette, Carol. *The Golden Forest*. Lanham, MA: Muddy Boots, 2021.
Read a story about a kelp forest ecosystem.

Fletcher, Patricia. *Kelp: The Underwater Forest!* New York, NY: Gareth Stevens, 2017.
Discover fascinating facts about kelp in this book.

Rhodes, Mary Jo, and David Hall. *Life in a Kelp Forest*. New York, NY: Scholastic, 2005.
This book explores what life is like in a kelp forest.

Websites

Britannica Kids: Seaweed
(https://kids.britannica.com/kids/article/seaweed/400176)
Read about seaweed basics.

Monterey Bay Aquarium: Kelp Forest!
(https://www.montereybayaquarium.org/animals/habitats/kelp-forest)
Readers can learn about amazing kelp forests.

The University of Maine: The Science of Seaweeds
(https://extension.umaine.edu/4h/stem-toolkits/the-science-of-seaweeds/#go-fish-for-seaweed)
Find out about the science of seaweeds.

INDEX

ABOUT THE AUTHOR

Joyce Markovics has written hundreds of books for kids. She lives in an old, creaky house along the Hudson River. She hopes the readers of this book will take action—in small and big ways—to protect nature, one of our greatest gifts. Joyce would like to thank Michael Graham, scientist and seaweed farmer, and his son Evan for their generous contributions to this book.